THE
HOLOCAUST

Susanna Davidson

Designed by Karen Tomlins

History consultant: Sir Martin Gilbert, CBE

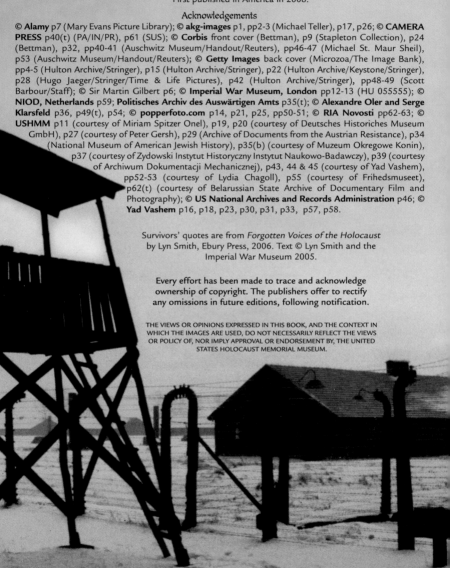

Edited by Jane Chisholm
Picture research by Ruth King

First published in 2008 by Usborne Publishing Ltd., Usborne House, 83-85 Saffron Hill,
London EC1N 8RT, England. www.usborne.com Copyright © 2008 Usborne Publishing Ltd.
The name Usborne and the devices ♀♀ are Trade Marks of Usborne Publishing Ltd.

Acknowledgements

© **Alamy** p7 (Mary Evans Picture Library); © **akg-images** p1, pp2-3 (Michael Teller), p17, p26; © **CAMERA
PRESS** p40(t) (PA/IN/PR), p61 (SUS); © **Corbis** front cover (Bettman), p9 (Stapleton Collection), p24
(Bettman), p32, pp40-41 (Auschwitz Museum/Handout/Reuters), pp46-47 (Michael St. Maur Sheil),
p53 (Auschwitz Museum/Handout/Reuters); © **Getty Images** back cover (Microzoa/The Image Bank),
pp4-5 (Hulton Archive/Stringer), p15 (Hulton Archive/Stringer), p22 (Hulton Archive/Keystone/Stringer),
p28 (Hugo Jaeger/Stringer/Time & Life Pictures), p42 (Hulton Archive/Stringer), pp48-49 (Scott
Barbour/Staff); © Sir Martin Gilbert p6; © **Imperial War Museum, London** pp12-13 (HU 055555); ©
NIOD, Netherlands p59; **Politisches Archiv des Auswärtigen Amts** p35(t); © **Alexandre Oler and Serge
Klarsfeld** p36, p49(t), p54; © **popperfoto.com** p14, p21, p25, pp50-51; © **RIA Novosti** pp62-63; ©
USHMM p11 (courtesy of Miriam Spitzer Onel), p19, p20 (courtesy of Deutsches Historiches Museum
GmbH), p27 (courtesy of Peter Gersh), p29 (Archive of Documents from the Austrian Resistance), p34
(National Museum of American Jewish History), p35(b) (courtesy of Muzeum Okregowe Konin),
p37 (courtesy of Zydowski Instytut Historyczny Instytut Naukowo-Badawczy), p39 (courtesy
of Archiwum Dokumentacji Mechanicznej), p43, 44 & 45 (courtesy of Yad Vashem),
pp52-53 (courtesy of Lydia Chagoll), p55 (courtesy of Frihedsmuseet), p62(t) (courtesy of Belarussian State Archive of Documentary Film and
Photography); © **US National Archives and Records Administration** p46; ©
Yad Vashem p16, p18, p23, p30, p31, p33, p57, p58.

Survivors' quotes are from *Forgotten Voices of the Holocaust*
by Lyn Smith, Ebury Press, 2006. Text © Lyn Smith and the
Imperial War Museum 2005.

Every effort has been made to trace and acknowledge
ownership of copyright. The publishers offer to rectify
any omissions in future editions, following notification.

THE VIEWS OR OPINIONS EXPRESSED IN THIS BOOK, AND THE CONTEXT IN
WHICH THE IMAGES ARE USED, DO NOT NECESSARILY REFLECT THE VIEWS
OR POLICY OF, NOR IMPLY APPROVAL OR ENDORSEMENT BY, THE UNITED
STATES HOLOCAUST MEMORIAL MUSEUM.

Contents

Chapter 1

What was the Holocaust?

In 1933, there were more than ten million Jews in Europe, but by 1945, six million had been murdered. In some countries, this meant a death toll of nine out of every ten Jews. This mass murder of Jewish people is now known as the Holocaust.

The force behind it was the Nazi Party, which came to power in Germany in January 1933. The Nazis, led by a man named Adolf Hitler, were

driven by the desire to create "a pure race" of people – blonde-haired, blue-eyed Germans, who would one day rule Europe. Only then would the Nazis Party's work be done.

From the moment Hitler came to power, he started a reign of terror against the Jews. Although they were his main victims, large numbers of Roma (Gypsies), Russians, Poles, Jehovah's Witnesses, homosexuals, disabled people and other so-called enemies of the Nazis were also imprisoned and killed. And, as the German army advanced across Europe, more and more people fell into the Nazis' hands – with terrible results.

A troop of German soldiers marches through a village in Romania. By 1941, the Nazis dominated most of Europe.

The Nazis didn't kill Jews because of their beliefs or for anything they had done. They murdered them simply because of who they were – because they were born Jewish.

While other groups suffered terribly under Hitler, the Jews were always the Nazis' main target. But why did the Nazis hate the Jews so much? How did they manage to kill so many people before they were stopped? The answer lies in hundreds of years of hatred.

This map shows the estimated number of Jews that were murdered in the areas conquered by Germany during the Second World War.

Chapter 2

Hatred

When Hitler came to power, there had been Jewish people living in Europe for 2,000 years. But still many people thought of them as outsiders, as not truly belonging to the countries in which they had made their homes. For the Jews originally came from the Middle East. They trace their roots back 3,000 years, when they were a tribe living in the Land of Canaan, now called Israel.

Here you can see Jews praying at the Western Wall in Israel. The wall is all that remains of the Second Temple built by Jews in Israel over 2,000 years ago.

The Jews had been forced out of their homeland in the year 70, after rebelling against Roman rule. They resettled all over the world – in the Middle East, North Africa and Europe. Even in these new lands, the Jews held on to a sense of themselves as a people. They were bound together not only by a shared culture, but also by their religion, Judaism, with its belief in one God.

At that time, however, a new religion was spreading across Europe. It was called Christianity, and its followers believed that a Jewish man, Jesus, was the son of God. Some early Christians blamed the Jews, not only for refusing to recognize Jesus as God's son, but also for his death. They didn't just hold the Jews of the time responsible – but every generation of Jews to come.

By the Middle Ages, it had become an unquestioned part of Christian teaching that the Jews were "Christ-killers" – agents of the devil who were plotting to bring down Christianity. Stories, without any truth in them, were told about Jews who killed Christian children and used their blood.

This German woodcut shows Jews being persecuted in Cologne in the late 14th century. They were forced into a pit, then burned alive.

Fear and hatred of the Jews meant that in some countries they were forced to live apart from the rest of the population, in gated areas, known as ghettos. In Venice, in Italy, Jews had to wear badges or hats so they could be instantly picked out; in Oxford, in England, they were forced to wear a yellow star.

In some countries, Jews chose to live in separate communities. They dressed differently to those around them, and Jews in Eastern Europe even spoke their own language, Yiddish. Thought of as "different" they were often treated with suspicion.

As a minority, the Jews also made easy scapegoats, or targets for blame. When a plague spread through Europe in the fourteenth century, people began to say that it was caused by Jews putting poison in the wells. Again and again, in times of trouble and unrest, Jews were either attacked or forced to leave their countries. In Spain, hundreds of Jews were burned at the stake if they refused to convert to Christianity.

"Eject them forever from this country," said the German preacher, Martin Luther, in 1543. "The blind Jews are truly stupid fools… wherever they have their synagogues, nothing is found but a den of devils."

For the Jews of Russia, life was particularly harsh. They suffered violent attacks, known as pogroms, in which the army and local people came together to destroy Jewish homes and beat up any Jews they could find. Between 1871 and 1905 there was a terrible wave of pogroms, and many Jews fled Russia, fearing for their lives.

Elsewhere in Europe, new ideas were taking hold about how all people should be treated equally.

As these ideas passed into law, Jews gradually found acceptance in the countries they called home. During the nineteenth and twentieth centuries, new jobs opened up to the Jews and the gates of the ghettos were pulled down.

Jews all over Europe began to lead very different lives. Some continued to hold onto the old traditions, but in many countries, particularly in Western Europe, more and more Jews entered into non-Jewish society. There were Jewish scientists, writers and musicians, Jewish bankers, businessmen, doctors and respected thinkers.

Two middle-class Jewish families, the Krassos and Spitzers, who were textile merchants, pose outside at a family gathering in Croatia.

But with success, came envy. In Germany, Austria and France, and throughout Eastern Europe, people spoke out against the Jews. Small political parties were formed, with the intention of forcing out the Jews once more.

Then, in 1914, the First World War broke out. By its end, four years later, many Jews were hopeful of more peaceful times ahead. Jewish men had fought for their countries, proving their loyalty. As one Czech Jewish schoolgirl, Edith Baneth, described her life at the time: "We were

This photograph, taken in 1919, shows Germans protesting about the land they had lost at the end of the First World War.

just citizens like anybody else. My parents had Jewish and non-Jewish friends and the idea that we should be different never entered my mind."

In Germany, however, the First World War was to leave deep scars. Germany had been on the losing side and the victors (Britain, France, Italy and the United States) forced the Germans to pay large sums of money to cover the damage done by German troops, and to give up huge swathes of land. German anger, frustration and resentment was soon to be felt all over Europe.

The posters read: "Danzig will always be ours!" and "Posen is German."

Chapter 3
The rise of the Nazis

After the First World War, life in Germany was very uncertain. Food was scarce, prices rose and small businesses went bankrupt. At such desperate times, people turned to extremes.

Adolf Hitler, a member of the National Socialist German Workers Party, known as the Nazi Party, took advantage of people's fears and disappointments. Continuing the tradition of using the Jews as scapegoats, he blamed them for Germany losing the war. He also made people feel good about being German again, claiming the

Germans, or "Aryans" as he called them, were the most superior people in the world. Beneath them were the Gypsies and the Slavic people of Eastern Europe.

Adolf Hitler, leader of the Nazi Party

Then, at the very bottom, were the Jews. "The Jews are undoubtedly a race, but not human..." he announced. "The Jews are an image of the devil."

At first, Hitler's Nazi Party only had a small following. But, in 1929, the German economy collapsed. Several million people lost their jobs and many turned against the government. Hitler's popularity rose, as people began to think of him as a strong and powerful figure who could solve Germany's problems. By 1930, the Nazi Party was the second largest and in January 1933, Hitler became the new leader of Germany.

Nazi Party members flying their flag with the black swastika symbol, at the National Socialist Party Day in January, 1933.

In Germany, 1933, members of the SA force Jews to march with signboards that read: "No upstanding German would buy from a Jew."

Once in power, Hitler moved quickly to silence anyone who might speak out against him. For support, he had a 400,000-strong army called the SA, as well as the blackshirted SS, a much-feared military force that worked as Hitler's personal bodyguard and beat up his opponents.

If the Jewish people of Germany hoped that Hitler's hatred of the Jews was just talk, they were quickly proven wrong. Four days after Hitler became leader, the first mass attacks on Jews took place in the streets in Germany. Groups of SA surrounded individual Jews and beat them up. In England, a newspaper described what happened. It told how many Jews were beaten, "until the blood streamed down their heads and faces... Many fainted and were left lying on the streets."

On the same day, Hitler ordered thousands of his political enemies, both Jews and non-Jews, to be sent to a camp, outside the town of Dachau. This was the first Nazi concentration camp. Inmates were held as prisoners and forced to live in terrible, cramped conditions, under the brutal control of the SS. Anyone who spoke out against Hitler risked being sent there.

From the moment the SS took over the running of the camps, they became known for their cruelty and violence, punishing prisoners with beatings, and in some cases, executions.

Prisoners from Dachau concentration camp on their way to work

On April 1, 1933, less than a month after their first attacks on Jews in Germany, the SA took to the streets once more. This time they were armed with pots of paints and brushes, as well as their guns and truncheons. They smeared the walls and doors of Jewish-owned businesses, shops and cafes. "Jews Out!" they wrote, or simply "Jew!"

The SA stopped anyone trying to enter Jewish shops. Those who refused were marked with a stamp on their faces that read: "We traitors bought at Jewish shops."

An SA soldier stands outside a Jewish shop in Berlin, with a sign that reads, "Germans! Beware! Don't buy from Jews!"

From that day on, Nazi attacks on the Jews were relentless. Law after law was passed banning Jews from all areas of everyday life – teaching in schools and universities, acting on stage, owning dogs, using public parks or swimming pools, working on newspapers, serving in the army... the list seemed endless.

Jews were banned from taking public transport, too. Here people stare out of a streetcar that is marked, "Forbidden to Jews."

The Nazis were also quick to move against other groups. Worried that people with disabilities would destroy the "purity" of the Aryan race, they passed a law in July 1933, allowing doctors to operate on disabled people, to stop them from having babies. Later, some Roma and Black people were operated on, too.

This is a propaganda poster for the Nuremberg Laws. It describes marriage between Jews and non-Jews as "race pollution" and warns against it.

Even though each new act made life more difficult for the Nazis' victims, many people still hoped that each act would be the last.

But in 1935, the Nazis issued the Nuremberg Laws, a set of laws that cut the Jews out of German life. The laws carefully defined who was Jewish, and who was not: a Jewish person was anyone with three grandparents who were born Jewish, or two grandparents who followed the Jewish faith.

The Nuremberg Laws also forbade marriage between Jews and non-Jews, and declared that from then on Jews were no longer German citizens. They were classed as "foreigners" with no laws to protect them, and no rights.

Jews could be fired from their jobs, have their businesses taken away from them, be beaten up in the street – and there was no one to whom they could turn for help.

Many Jews fled from Hitler's Germany, choosing to leave their homes and their friends rather than face Nazi cruelty. Most went to nearby European countries, including France and Belgium, although some went as far afield as the United States, Australia, India and Palestine (the future Israel).

A member of the Nazi party measures the nose of a man he suspects is Jewish. The Nazis wrongly believed you could identify Jews by the size of their features.

But the Jews who settled in Europe were still not safe. Hitler's long-term plan was to conquer the land Germany had lost in the First World War – and more besides. He wanted to create a new empire for the German people, and for this he needed more land, which he called "living space" – *Lebensraum*. In this new empire, there would be no room for Jews.

In March 1938, Hitler came a step closer to his dream, when German forces entered Austria. Anti-Jewish laws were immediately brought into effect and Austrian Jews were beaten up and humiliated on the streets.

This photograph, taken in August 1938, shows a group of elderly Jewish men being forced to scrub the streets of Vienna as German officers look on.

Tens of thousands more Jews fled Nazi rule, but they were forced to leave behind all their belongings, and even had to pay money to leave the country. Those without friends or family abroad faced poverty if they decided to leave, and the difficulty of building a new life from scratch.

Some told themselves that things would get better, but in November 1938 events took an even more violent turn. A young Jewish man, whose parents had been driven out of Germany, shot a German diplomat. The Nazis used this as an excuse to go on the rampage. They set fire to 1,000 synagogues, destroyed Jewish-owned shops and killed more than 90 Jews. There was so much shattered glass on the streets it became known as *Kristallnacht* – The Night of the Broken Glass.

Wiesbaden synagogue burning on *Kristallnacht*, November 9, 1938

After that, more Jews than ever wanted to leave. But governments of foreign countries were worried about their own problems of unemployment, as well as the risk of sparking off anti-Jewish feelings. So they either refused entry to Jews or set strict limits on the numbers they would take.

Things had become much worse for the Nazis' other victims, too. In 1936, the Nuremberg Laws were extended to include Black people and Roma. Then, in 1938, four months before *Kristallnacht*, hundreds of Roma throughout Germany and Austria were rounded up as part of a "Gypsy clean-up week" and sent to concentration camps. And the Roma, like the Jews, found it difficult to escape Germany. Other countries would not let them in.

German-Jewish refugees arrive in Belgium, in June 1939. The ship had first tried to go to Cuba and the US, but the refugees had been denied entry by the authorities.

Some Jewish parents, who could not find a way to leave Germany, sent their children to Britain on ships as part of *Kindertransport*, a plan set up to evacuate children out of Nazi Germany. 9,354 children were saved this way. Most never saw their parents again.

This Jewish girl has come to England from Austria, on a boat called *The Prague*. There were 502 children on board, all sent away by their parents to escape the Nazis.

The following year, 1939, it looked as if the world was heading for war once more. Hitler invaded Czechoslovakia in March, and other nations vowed that if he invaded one more country, they would take military action against him.

Ignoring their warnings, Hitler invaded Poland in September. Britain and France responded by declaring war. From that moment on, borders closed and the Jews of Europe were trapped. It then became a question of waiting, and seeing what happened next.

Chapter 4

The world at war

In January 1939, Hitler had predicted what would happen if there was another world war. He said the outcome would be, "the annihilation of the Jewish race in Europe." But, as yet, he had no detailed plans for getting rid of the Jews.

Over the next two years, the German army seemed unstoppable. Every country it invaded crumbled before it. By the summer of 1940, Germany controlled all the land from France to Poland. Millions of Jews came under Nazi rule.

The red markings on this map show the German advance across Europe by 1942.

In Western Europe, the Nazis didn't move against the Jews immediately, lulling them into thinking they might still be safe. But in the East it was a different story.

Here German soldiers round up a group of Jewish men in Poland, in 1939.

In Poland, groups of SS men roamed through towns, burning synagogues and shooting dead anyone who tried to escape. They kicked Jews in public and laughed about it – to them it was a kind of game. At any time, Jewish people could be snatched from their homes and sent to work camps, where they had to slave away, far from their homes, under the brutal guard of the SS.

Thousands of non-Jewish Poles were killed too. All those in positions of authority – mayors, priests, teachers, lawyers – were shot on the streets or sent to work camps. Hitler thought that removing these people would make it easier to control the country.

A group of Jewish children pose in front of a makeshift shelter in the Kutno Ghetto, Poland, in early 1940. In June that year, the Germans surrounded the area with barbed wire and watchtowers.

While random killings were taking place on the streets, an SS general named Reinhard Heydrich gave orders for all the Jews in Poland to be identified, rounded up and confined in ghettos in towns – just like Jews in the Middle Ages. The ghettos were surrounded by walls, barbed wire and armed guards, and the Jews inside were made to work, like slaves, for German needs.

The first ghetto was created in the town of Piotrkow, in Poland, in October 1939. Forty more soon followed. The Nazis demanded that each ghetto was run by Councils of Jews, who had to manage the ghettos and carry out Nazi orders.

More and more Jews were expelled from their homes, until the ghettos were horrifically overcrowded. There was not enough food, and in the cramped conditions, diseases spread. The Jews set up schools and put on plays to try to keep spirits up, but they couldn't win the battle for survival. 12,000 Jews would die from starvation in the Lodz ghetto in one year alone.

In 1940, German Roma were also sent to the ghettos. They were kept in separate areas but made to live in the same terrible conditions.

Worse was to come. In June 1941, German troops invaded the Soviet Union. In their wake came the SS killing squads. Their task was to destroy every Jewish community, and any Roma, they came across.

Police rounding up Roma families in Vienna, ready for deportation to the ghettos in Poland

This photograph, taken in 1941, shows a group of Jewish women being forced to strip, shortly before their death by firing squad.

Men, women and children were driven from their homes, then forced to walk at gunpoint to pits a few miles away, which had been dug only a few hours earlier. Everyone was ordered to undress and then shot, so the bodies tumbled into the ready-made graves. Within twelve months, more than one million Jews had been killed in this way.

As in other parts of Europe, the Nazis needed help from the local population to carry out its actions against the Jews. Drawing on centuries of anti-Jewish feelings, the SS squads used local volunteers to help carry out the shootings.

The plans to "do away" with the Jews were stepped up in late 1941, when Hitler authorized the rounding up Jews from Germany, Austria and Czechoslovakia. Under his orders, they were to be sent by train to the Polish ghettos and to other cities in the East – Minsk, Kovno and Riga.

Upon arriving in Riga, some Jews were sent on to work camps in the region, while others were put into a new ghetto set up for German Jews. Those sent to Minsk and Kovno were taken from the train to isolated areas nearby, and then shot.

This first deportation of the Jews to the East continued until February 1942, by which time thousands upon thousands of Jewish homes were left empty, their inhabitants gone forever.

Here, German soldiers are rounding up Romanian Jews and forcing them from their homes. Families took all the belongings they could, not knowing where they were going.

Heinrich Himmler, the man in charge of the creation of the death camps

Still, the Nazis were not satisfied. Even as Jewish people died of starvation and disease in the ghettos and were murdered in their thousands by the killing squads, the Chief of the SS, Heinrich Himmler, was planning a third way to get rid of the Jews: murder by poison gas. This was what the Nazis called the "Final Solution" to the Jewish Question.

Tragically, at this time, many Jews were filled with hope that the war would soon end, and that Hitler would be stopped. In December 1941, the United States had entered the war on the side of Britain. "Most people believe the war will not last long now," a Jewish girl in the Warsaw Ghetto, Mary Berg, noted in her diary. America's entry into the war, she added, "has inspired the hundreds of thousands of dejected Jews in the ghetto with a new breath of hope."

Within a year of her writing these words, thousands of Jews were being gassed to death daily. Under the cover of war, the Nazis had forged ahead with their plan to wipe out an entire people.

Murder by gas had first been tried out on Germans, on Hitler's orders, in 1939, on the very sick and the disabled, including thousands of children. Later, it was used on Roma and Russian prisoners of war.

The first gassing of Jews took place near Chelmno, a remote village in German-occupied Poland, in December 1941. Having been told they were being taken to work in Germany, local men and women were driven in batches of eighty in a special van to the Chelmno woods. By the time the journey was over all were dead, gassed by exhaust fumes pumped back into the van.

These Jews died without even their names being recorded. They had become, in Nazi eyes, vermin to be exterminated.

One of the gas vans at Chelmno, used to kill Jews and Roma

A group of Jewish men and women gather on the station platform, as they are deported from the Lodz ghetto to Chelmno death camp.

On January 22, 1942, at a villa on the shores of the Wannsee lake in Germany, SS General Reinhard Heydrich laid out plans for the complete destruction of the Jews.

Europe was to be combed from East to West: Jews were to be forced into ghettos, and from there they would be taken by train to work camps further East. The work was expected to be so harsh, and the conditions so awful, that a large number would "fall away" – meaning that they would die. Those who were not fit for work, "will have to be dealt with appropriately," said Heydrich.

Plans for these Jews were already in place. They would be sent to death camps, and gassed to death in specially built chambers, except at Chelmno, where gas vans were still in use. The bodies were then burned, or buried in mass graves, leaving no trace of the people who had been murdered.

Land	Zahl
A. Altreich	131.800
Ostmark	43.700
Ostgebiete	420.000
Generalgouvernement	2.284.000
Bialystok	400.000
Protektorat Böhmen und Mähren	74.200
Estland - Judenfrei -	
Lettland	
Litauen	
Belgien	3.500
Dänemark	34.000
Frankreich / Besetztes Gebiet	43.000
Unbesetztes Gebiet	5.600
Griechenland	165.000
Niederlande	700.000
Norwegen	69.600
	1.300
B. Bulgarien	48.000
England	330.000
Finnland	2.300
Irland	4.000
Italien einschl. Sardinien	58.000
Albanien	200
Kroatien	40.000
Portugal	3.000
Rumänien einschl. Bessarabien	342.000
Schweden	8.000
Schweiz	18.000
Serbien	10.000
Slowakei	88.000
Spanien	6.000
Türkei (europ. Teil)	55.500
Ungarn	742.800
UdSSR	5.000.000
Ukraine	2.994.684
Weißrußland aus- schl. Bialystok	446.484
Zusammen: über	11.000.000

This list, presented at the Wannsee Conference, shows the number of Jews in each country that the Nazis estimated they would have to kill to achieve their Final Solution.

This photograph shows all that was left of the Jews gassed at Chelmno: their belongings, stored in a nearby synagogue.

Chapter 5

The business of death

There were four death camps at first: Chelmno, Belzec, Sobibor and Treblinka, all in German-occupied Poland. The sites had been carefully chosen, both for their remoteness, and for the fact they could easily be reached by rail.

The first victims came by train from the ghettos in Western Poland. The deportations began in December 1941. By early 1943 the ghettos were all but emptied.

When the transports arrived, a few men were chosen as workers, known as *Sonderkommandos*. Everyone else – men, women and children – was sent straight to their deaths. Two

'Gassing', a painting by Auschwitz survivor David Olère, depicting the gas chambers

million Jews, and tens of thousands of Roma, were gassed to death at these camps.

The SS ordered the Jewish Councils to select Jews for deportation. The members of the Councils were often despised for agreeing to work with the Germans. But a few Council leaders believed they would be able to save people – that by handing over the old and the weak for deportation, they could keep the young alive as a workforce for the Nazi war effort. Others realized the deception though. When the head of the Warsaw Council, Adam Czerniakow, was ordered to hand over 4,000 Jews for deportation, he killed himself.

Adam Czerniakow, second from left, with a girl he succeeded in freeing after German guards arrested her for smuggling bread into the ghetto.

Most Council leaders didn't know exactly where their fellow Jews were being taken. The Nazis told them they were being sent to work camps or to farms in the East. But fear lurked in everyone's minds that they were being taken to their deaths.

When it was time for the selections, mothers and fathers would try to hide their children wherever they could. Adam Adams, a Polish Jew, remembered what it was like when the SS came into his house in the ghetto, looking for Jews in hiding. "They would come into the room shouting and shooting... I cannot describe to you... Imagine, winter nights, suddenly you hear noises, voices, you hear shooting, the fear is indescribable and the running, everyone scrambling..."

Because most people who were deported to the death camps were killed immediately, there are very few accounts of what it was like there. Of the 600,000 Jews deported to Belzec, for example, only two survived. One of those, Chaim Hirszman, recalled how, "We were told to undress before we go to the bath... After undressing we were told to form two groups, one of men and the other of women with children. An SS man, with the strike of a horsewhip, sent the men to the right or the left, to death or to work."

Hirszman was selected to work. It would be his job to carry the bodies of the dead out of the gas chamber. He then had to shave off their hair, which was packed into sacks and sent to Germany, where it was used to make felt or yarn. He recalled how in one of the "transports" taken out of the gas chamber, he found the body of his own wife and had to shave her hair.

A group of Roma prisoners await instructions from the German guards, inside Belzec concentration camp.

An aerial view of Auschwitz-Birkenau, showing the barracks where the prisoners lived

In the spring of 1942, a fifth camp was set up – Birkenau. It was next to a camp called Auschwitz, which until now had held Polish political prisoners. Auschwitz-Birkenau was different from the other camps, as it functioned both as a work and a death camp. One other camp, Majdanek, operated along the same lines.

Auschwitz-Birkenau was to become the largest camp of them all, where the most Jews were

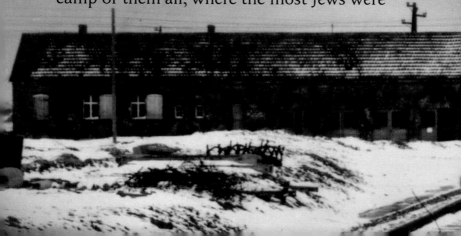

murdered. But more people were to survive it than the four death camps, as the strongest and fittest could survive by being selected for work.

The camp lay on a main railway junction with direct links to every capital in Europe. Until the end of 1944, Jewish men, women and children, as well as Roma, were brought to Auschwitz from concentration camps all over Europe.

The train journeys were long, some taking several days, and the conditions were terrible. "The stench in that train!" Barbara Stimler, a young Polish Jewish woman remembered. "I cannot tell you. It's *impossible* to visualize. We were like animals." Often with no food or water, many died on the journey itself.

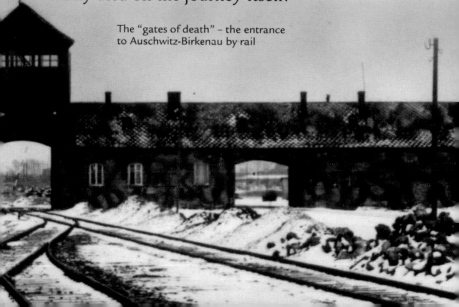

The "gates of death" – the entrance to Auschwitz-Birkenau by rail

A group of Hungarian prisoners spill out of a German boxcar onto the crowded station platform at Auschwitz.

As the train drew into the camp, the doors were thrown open and the guards screamed, "Out! Out! Out!" No one knew what was happening. The Nazis deceived the prisoners until the last possible moment, trying to keep them calm and under control.

A selection was then made on the station platform. All those considered "unfit" for work, as the Nazis termed it, were ordered into trucks. They were mostly made up of the old and the very young, women with babies and children without mothers. The Nazis told them they would be washed and given food. Instead, they went straight to the gas chambers.

Those considered "fit" for work were divided into groups of men and women and sent to the barracks at Birkenau. From there, they were sent out daily to work camps in the area.

These life or death decisions were made by SS doctors, including Dr. Mengele, who became a much-feared figure. He would stand on the station platform, in his spotless uniform and white gloves. With a flick of his finger, he decided the fate of every person that arrived.

Jews from Hungary undergo the selection process on the platform at Auschwitz-Birkenau. The men in the striped clothes are Jewish prisoners, known as *kapos*, whose job was to collect the belongings.

Unknown to them, these Jewish-Hungarian women and children have been selected for death, and are on their way to the gas chambers at Auschwitz-Birkenau.

Those chosen to live were ordered to strip, shower and were then shaved. A young Jewish boy from Poland, Roman Halter, remembered how, "There was a big trough of disinfectant which looked like iodine and we had to submerge ourselves in that. If we didn't submerge fully, SS guards would stand on us with their boots until even our heads were submerged."

After being shaved, everyone was given a bundle of mismatched clothes, taken from those who had already been killed. Helen Pelc, a young

Polish woman, remembered being given wooden clogs and a dress that was so long she couldn't walk in it. "I was calling for my mother," she recalled. "I hardly recognized her, nor her me because we had no hair; and I had a lovely head of red hair!"

Finally, everyone filed through another room, where a number was tattooed on their arms. From that moment on they were no longer people with names – just prisoners with numbers, who would be treated worse than animals. As soon as any of them became too weak to work, they too would be sent to the gas chambers.

A group of Jewish-Hungarian women who have been selected for work at Auschwitz-Birkenau. They are marching to their barracks after disinfection and having their heads shaved.

That first night in the barracks, everyone was filled with confusion. The new arrivals still did not know exactly what the Nazis were doing to the Jews. Anna Bergman, who had been deported to Auschwitz from Czechoslovakia, remembered how her friend asked the others in the barrack where her parents were, as they had been sent to the other side during the selection. The others all started screaming with laughter. "You stupid idiot," they told her friend, "they are all up the chimney now." Anna remembered how she thought they were insane, and they thought she was.

A photograph of the ovens in the crematoria. This is where the bodies were burned after being gassed.

The largest room in the crematoria at Auschwitz, where the dead bodies were stored. It was later converted into a gas chamber.

Camp life at Auschwitz-Birkenau was strictly controlled. Everyone knew they could be killed at any moment – for the smallest thing, or for nothing at all, or if they simply became too weak for work. The smell of burning bodies from the chimneys of the crematoria hung in the air as a constant reminder. "You were breathing in the dead," said Jan Hartman, an Auschwitz survivor.

All the camps were surrounded by electrified barbed-wire fences, a chain of watchtowers and guards armed with machine guns. There was also a roll call every morning, to make sure no one had escaped. Inmates would have to stand for hours, often in freezing conditions, while numbers were called out. Then everyone was divided into work groups, known as *Kommandos*, and forced to march, often at a run, to the place where they worked.

Which *Kommando* you were in could be a matter of life or death. A job in the kitchens could save your life, as you could then steal scraps of food while you worked.

This drawing by David Olère, entitled 'Leaving for Work', shows prisoners being marched to work past victims of camp discipline.

The many factories around Auschwitz were owned by German companies, who wanted to take advantage of the slave work on offer. The latest technology was used in building the factories, but less care was taken with the workforce. The factories were run by members of the SS, who treated the workers so brutally that more than half of them died.

These are the watchtowers and high voltage fences that surrounded Auschwitz-Birkenau, to stop prisoners from escaping.

The same harsh treatment was true of the other work camps, which existed throughout Nazi-occupied Europe. Once the work was finished, the factory would be shut down, and the camp liquidated. Those who were still fit enough to work might be sent on to another work camp; those who had lost their strength were killed outright.

Premysl Dobias, a survivor of Mauthausen concentration camp, remembered what it was like to work there. He described the journey they took every day from the camp to the granite quarry.

Prisoners from the German concentration camp at Sachsenhausen at work in a quarry. Their back-breaking job was to make the huge boulders into small stones.

"We had to run so fast that most of us lost our clogs and had to run barefoot on awfully sharp granite stones which were so painful that we screamed with pain. Our feet were bleeding and many of us got infections from the dirt and very soon died. When we came to the top of the steps, down at intervals were the SS and as we passed they were hitting us."

The Nazis also made money from the dead. Clothes taken from the Jews were sent to Germany and handed out to civilians. Unaware of where the clothes had come from, some wrote in and complained about bloodstained items.

At Auschwitz-Birkenau, a special section of the camp was set aside to house the belongings of those who had just arrived. The area was known by the Jews who worked there as "Canada" – the land of wealth and plenty.

By 1943, the Nazis had made the business of death into a cruel science. There was to be no waste. Even the ashes from the burned bodies were put to use – as fertilizer on the nearby fields.

A photograph of "Canada" – one of the huge warehouses where the belongings of gassed prisoners were stored

Chapter 6
Fighting back

For those in the ghettos or concentration camps, just to live was a daily struggle against hunger and despair. Anyone who gave up hope did not last long. That was what the Nazis wanted. Survival itself became a form of resistance.

Some found it easier to cope if they formed groups of friends, looking out for each other and talking together about their lives before the war. Mothers did all they could to protect their daughters; fathers their sons.

This shows the women's barracks at Auschwitz. Prisoners lived in overcrowded conditions and slept on hard wooden bunks.

A self-portrait by David Olère, showing food he found abandoned near the crematoria, which he then threw over the fence to the prisoners in the women's camp.

Others looked out for themselves, stealing food or bartering goods on the camps' black markets.

There were also thousands of small acts of resistance. In the factories, workers would try to sabotage Nazi goods. They would work slowly, break machines, damage parts.

Those who were caught faced death by hanging. But even this last act could be turned into one of retaliation. One Austrian boy at Auschwitz, Freddie Knoller, recalled, "The three boys came pale-faced out of the bunker with their hands tied at the back. They were marched to the gallows and we all had to stand at attention and watch them...

The amazing thing is that one of them was courageous enough to shout, 'Long live liberty!'.... The SS man who opened the trap door got all red in the face... the trap door opened and the three boys were hanged. This defiance gave us courage."

Outside the camps, there were many instances of non-Jews risking their lives to save Jews. In Denmark, the entire country came together to help the Jews. At the beginning of October 1943, the Nazis planned to deport all of Denmark's Jews to concentration camps. Warned in advance by a courageous German, the Danes ferried the Jews across the sea to safety in Sweden. More than 7,000 people were saved this way.

Danish-Jewish children in a children's home in Sweden, after their escape from Denmark

There were also brave non-Jews who gave Jewish families a place to hide and provided them with food, even though to be caught could mean death. Thousands of Jews, particularly Jewish children, were saved this way. They spent the war cooped up in tiny spaces: cellars, attics, barns, relying on friends or contacts to bring them food.

Some only had themselves to rely on. Ania Shore hid in a hayloft in Poland: "We had to whisper – for two and a half years we never spoke once above a whisper! Nor could we go out in the daytime. We were hanging on to life by a thin thread, always cold, scared of shadows, running, listening."

Many Jews who managed to escape the Nazis joined up with resistance movements, or formed their own. The forests of Poland were home to several different groups. Some had extensive hideouts from which they planned attacks on the Germans, and gave shelter to those who escaped from the ghettos.

In France, a group known as the Jewish Army attacked German military trucks and factories, while in Belgium a group managed to derail a train on its way to Auschwitz, enabling several hundred Jews to escape.

Rebellion and revolt also took place inside the ghettos. In April and May 1943, the last remaining inhabitants of the Warsaw Ghetto rose up in arms against the SS as they came in to deport them. The Germans had 135 machine guns, the Jews had two. The Germans had 1,358 rifles, the Jews had fifteen. Their main weapons were grenades and petrol bombs, but for a whole month they were able to hold out against the Germans, before being viciously crushed.

In this photograph from the Warsaw Ghetto Uprising, a Jewish man leaps to his death from a burning building, rather than face capture by the Germans.

"Jewish armed resistance and retaliation have become a reality," wrote Mordechai Anielewicz, commander of the uprising, shortly before he was killed in the fighting. "I have been witness to the magnificent heroic struggle of the Jewish fighters."

There were even revolts in the death camps. On August 2, 1943, Jewish workers at Treblinka set fire to the camp and fought their way out. Only a few escaped, but as a result of the rebels' courage, the Nazis' operation at Treblinka was over.

The superior strength of the Nazis meant that those who fought back rarely survived. But resistance was a chance to show defiance. As a poster inside the Warsaw Ghetto put it, they were prepared to, "Fight for life to the last breath."

These Jewish fighters from the United Partisan Organization helped Jews in the Vilna Ghetto from their base in a nearby forest. They obtained weapons, forged documents for fellow Jews, and mined railroad tracks.

Chapter 7

The killing continues

By mid-1943, the Germans were beginning to lose the war. They had invaded Russia two years earlier, and were feeling the full force of the immense Russian army, as well as being pushed back first in North Africa and then in Italy.

But the Nazis refused to let that interfere with their plans for the Jews. More trains than ever were reaching Auschwitz each day, carrying Jews from all the corners of Europe.

This photograph shows 180 Dutch Jews leaving Westerbork, a transit camp in Holland, in a train bound for Auschwitz.

Sensing that time was running out, the Nazis stepped up the speed of their Final Solution. In May 1944, they began deportations from Hungary, which they had occupied only two months earlier. As many as three trains left Hungary every day for more than 50 days. They were headed for Auschwitz-Birkenau, where the death rate reached 12,000 a day. Within two months, the Nazis managed to kill two-thirds of the Jews of Hungary.

Meanwhile, the Russian army was drawing ever closer to the camps in German-occupied Poland. In response, the Nazis began to evacuate the camps, blowing up the gas chambers in an attempt to hide their crimes. Prisoners in work camps were forced to march westward, to factories and concentration camps in Germany. Many marches began on foot. Those who were too weak, or who fell behind, were shot. An estimated 100,000 Jews died on these death marches.

Even as the war effort was collapsing, the Nazis single-mindedly pursued their plan to wipe out the Jews. In April 1945, the Russian army closed in on Berlin, the German capital. Aware he had lost the war, Hitler committed suicide. That same day, a thousand Jews on a death march to Czechoslovakia were shot by their guards.

The soldiers who entered the camps were faced with an unimaginable sight. Many of the survivors were skeletal. One British soldier, Peter Coombs, wrote to his wife, "I see their corpses lying near their hovels, for they crawl or totter out into the sunlight to die. I watched them make their last feeble journeys, and even as I watched they died."

This Hungarian Jew, photographed after the liberation of Belsen Concentration Camp on April 15, 1945, was one of the few still able to walk.

Survivors at Auschwitz greet their liberators in January, 1945.

Even for those who survived, the struggle was far from over. Most discovered they were the only members of their family still alive. As one survivor, Anna Bergman, described her return home, "All through the years you had to keep fighting... But now, you realized there is nobody here and nothing, and what do you do now?"

Afterword

Remembering

The Holocaust is an almost impossible event to take in. All over Europe, Jewish communities were wiped out, a whole way of life was destroyed. The numbers, too, are so huge – six million dead. But sometimes just a piece of someone's story, a letter, a photograph, reveals the human face behind a number, with a life that was stolen or changed forever.

Looking back on the Holocaust, there are so many questions. How could it have happened? Who knew about it? Why didn't more people try to stop it? Perhaps now, the most important thing, is to make sure it is not forgotten.

A funeral held for all the bodies found at Auschwitz. Local people and German prisoners of war were made to help carry the coffins.

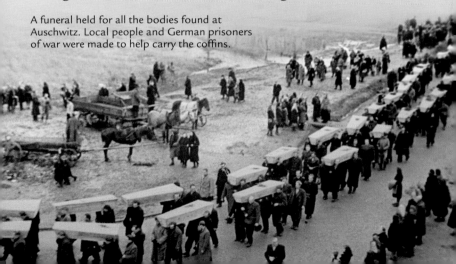

Internet links

You can find out more about the Holocaust by going to the Usborne Quicklinks Website. Here we have provided links to sites where you can see video footage of what life was like for Jews before the Holocaust, listen to survivors' stories and look at photographs taken inside the ghettos and concentration camps.

For links to these sites, go to the Usborne Quicklinks Website at www.usborne-quicklinks.com and enter the keyword *holocaust*.

When using the Internet, please follow the Internet safety guidelines shown on the Usborne Quicklinks Website. The links at Usborne Quicklinks are regularly reviewed and updated, but Usborne Publishing is not responsible and does not accept liability for the content of any website other than its own. We recommend that children are surpervised while on the Internet.

Index